Public Speaking Materials and Resources

Communication Studies 20

4th Edition

Department of Communications Studies,
San Jose State University

Australia • Brazil • Japan • Korea • Mexico • Singapore • Spain • United Kingdom • United States

**Public Speaking Materials and Resources:
Communication Studies 20, 4th Edition**

Department of Communications Studies, San Jose
State University

Executive Editors:
Michele Baird

Maureen Staudt

Michael Stranz

Project Development Manager:
Linda deStefano

Senior Marketing Coordinators:
Sara Mercurio

Lindsay Shapiro

Senior Production / Manufacturing Manager:
Donna M. Brown

PreMedia Services Supervisor:
Rebecca A. Walker

Rights & Permissions Specialist:
Kalina Hintz

Cover Image:
Getty Images*

© 2009, 2005 Department of Communications Studies,
San Jose State University

Photo Credit for front cover image by Janet Sundrud

For product information and technology assistance, contact us at
Cengage Learning Customer & Sales Support, 1-800-354-9706

For permission to use material from this text or product,
submit all requests online at **cengage.com/permissions**
Further permissions questions can be emailed to
permissionrequest@cengage.com

ISBN-13: 978-1-4266-4752-9

ISBN-10: 1-4266-4752-2

Cengage Learning
5191 Natorp Boulevard
Mason, Ohio 45040
USA

Cengage Learning is a leading provider of customized learning solutions with
office locations around the globe, including Singapore, the United Kingdom,
Australia, Mexico, Brazil, and Japan. Locate your local office at:
international.cengage.com/region

Cengage Learning products are represented in Canada by Nelson Education, Ltd.

For your lifelong learning solutions, visit **custom.cengage.com**

Visit our corporate website at **cengage.com**

Printed in the United States of America

Communication Studies 20:

Public Speaking

Course Packet

Table of Contents

Part I: Getting Started

Part II: Demonstration Speech

Part III: Informative Speech

Part IV: Persuasive Speech

Part V: Activities and Engagements

Communication Studies is a vibrant and growing major at SJSU! Students begin with coursework in critical thinking and advocacy and then continue on to other more specialized subjects, including health communication, intercultural communication, instructional communication, organizational communication, performance studies, media criticism and rhetoric.

To learn more, or for more information about the Department of Communication Studies, contact: Dr. Dennis Jaehne, Department Chair; (408) 924-5360 or visit http://www.sjsu.edu/depts/commstudies/

For more information about Comm 20: Public Speaking at San José State University contact: Dr. Deanna L. Fassett, Department of Communication Studies, (408) 924-5511; Deanna.Fassett@sjsu.edu

Packet materials revised by Roxanne Cnudde and Deanna L. Fassett. Cover photo taken by Janet Sundrud. Department logo created by Hugh Haiker.

Student Information Sheet

Name:

Year in school:

Major:

E-mail address:

Public speaking experience:

What helps you learn?

How comfortable are you speaking in front of a group?

How familiar are you with outlining?

How familiar are you with the SJSU library?

What are your areas of interest? Hobbies?

What other commitments do you have outside of school (work, volunteering, etc.)?

Please share any additional information you feel I should know:

Helpful SJSU Campus Resources

Communication Studies Lab and Resource Center

Nervous about public speaking? Want help developing your communication skills? The Lab offers support (e.g., drop-in assistance, self-paced instructional modules, and workshops) for students enrolled in all Communication Studies classes. You can even earn credit by enrolling in COMM 80; completing just three activities means an extra unit for you! For more information, please contact the Lab Director, Beth Von Till (408-924-5384), or Assistant Director, Liz Harris (408-924-5395). Located in Clark Hall Room 240. URL: http://www.sjsu.edu/depts/commstudies/lab/index.html

The Writing Center is an instructional resource for all students of all disciplines and writing abilities. They offer tutoring and workshops tailored to the needs of individuals and groups. Located in Clark Hall Suite 126. URL: http://www.sjsu.edu/writingcenter/

The Learning Assistance Resource Center (LARC) is designed to assist students in the development of their full academic potential and to motivate them to become self-directed learners. The center provides support services, such as skills assessment, individual or group tutorials, subject advising, learning assistance, summer academic preparation and basic skills development. Located in the Student Services Center, room 600. URL: http://www.sjsu.edu/larc/

The Peer Mentor Program is designed to help ease the transition to SJSU by empowering students to help each other and themselves. Peer Mentors are among the best, brightest, and most diverse SJSU students. Peer Mentors facilitate discussions on academic coping skills (e.g., how to approach assignments, talk to a professor, use technology, or pick a major) and other student concerns (e.g., stress and time management, living in the residence halls, dealing with parents, food, exercise, gaming and the internet, finding resources on campus, making friends, and dating). Peer Mentors are in the MUSE classrooms as well as available in the Peer Mentor Center located in the Academic Success Center in Clark Hall. URL: http://www.sjsu.edu/muse/peermentor/

Public Speaking Ethics

As a speaker:

- Choose a topic that is relevant to your audience and that you think has ethically sound goals.

- Think through the implications of your speech topic for your audience.

- Be fully prepared for your speech. KNOW your topic thoroughly.

- Do all you can to learn about your audience and then develop your speech for them.

- Never use fallacies or name calling.

- Utilize the public forum for quality discussion of important issues, not to slander.

- Be a model for quality public discussion that focuses on issues.

- Always be respectful of the titles and group designations by which people prefer to be identified.

As an audience member (listener):

- Be open as a listener.

- Give the speaker enough time to present his/her point completely before you jump to conclusions.

- Address the speaker respectfully.

- Address the issues at hand, not the character of the speaker.

Research:

- Always be honest and truthful about your data and your interpretation of the data. Think through your interpretations very carefully and consider multiple sides.

- Always research multiple sides of an issue. You cannot ethically argue for one side or another without having a clear picture and a thorough understanding of what the other sides represent.

- Acknowledge counter arguments whenever it seems appropriate. Never mislead your audience by withholding vital information.

- Trust the audience members to ultimately know what is in their own best interest. Give them the most information you can, set up your arguments to the best of your ability, and then let them decide.

- Always, always, always, cite your sources in your outlines. Cite them in your speech whenever necessary. Otherwise, it is plagiarism.

Multicultural Ground Rules
for a Public Speaking class

- Our primary commitment is to learn from the instructor, from each other, from materials and from our work. We acknowledge differences amongst us in skills, interests, values, scholarly orientations and experience.

- We acknowledge that racism, sexism, ageism, heterosexism, ableism, classism, theism, and other forms of discrimination exist and are likely to surface from time to time.

- We acknowledge that one of the meanings of racism is that we have been systematically taught misinformation about our own group and especially members of devalued groups and populations of color (this is true for both dominant and dominated group members). The same is true about other "isms"—we are taught misinformation about ourselves and others regarding forms of difference and discrimination.

- We cannot be blamed for the misinformation we have heard but we will be held responsible for repeating misinformation after we have learned otherwise.

- We will not blame victims for their oppression.

- We will assume that people are always doing the best they can, both to learn the material and to behave in non-racist, non-sexist, non-classist, non-heterosexist, and multiculturally sensitive ways.

- We will actively pursue opportunities to learn about our own groups and those of others, yet not enter or invade others' privacy when unwanted.

- We will share information about our groups with other students, and we will not demean, devalue, or "put down" people for their experiences or lifestyles.

- We each have an obligation to actively combat the myths and stereotypes about our own groups and other groups so that we can break down the walls that hinder group cooperation and group gain.

- We will work toward creating a safe atmosphere for open discussion. Thus, at times, someone may wish to make a comment that s/he does not want repeated outside this class. If so, the person will preface the remarks with a request and we will agree to not repeat the remarks.

Personal Report of Communication Apprehension 24

This instrument is composed of twenty-four statements concerning feelings about communicating with others. Please indicate the degree to which each statement applies to you by marking whether you:

Strongly Agree	Agree	Neutral	Disagree	Strongly Disagree
1	2	3	4	5

_____1. I dislike participating in group discussions.

_____2. Generally, I am comfortable while participating in group discussions.

_____3. I am tense and nervous while participating in group discussions.

_____4. I like to get involved in group discussions.

_____5. Engaging in a group discussion with new people makes me tense and nervous.

_____6. I am calm and relaxed while participating in group discussions.

_____7. Generally, I am nervous when I have to participate in a meeting.

_____8. Usually, I am comfortable when I have to participate in a meeting.

_____9. I am very calm and relaxed when I am called upon to express an opinion at a meeting.

_____10. I am afraid to express myself at meetings.

_____11. Communicating at meetings usually makes me uncomfortable.

_____12. I am very relaxed when answering questions at a meeting.

_____13. While participating in a conversation with a new acquaintance, I feel very nervous.

_____14. I have no fear of speaking up in conversations.

_____15. Ordinarily I am very tense and nervous in conversations.

_____16. Ordinarily I am very calm and relaxed in conversations.

_____17. While conversing with a new acquaintance, I feel very relaxed.

_____18. I'm afraid to speak up in conversations.

_____19. I have no fear of giving a speech.

_____20. Certain parts of my body feel very tense and rigid while giving a speech.

_____21. I feel relaxed while giving a speech.

_____22. My thoughts become confused and jumbled when I am giving a speech.

_____23. I face the prospect of giving a speech with confidence.

_____24. While giving a speech, I get so nervous I forget facts I really know.

SCORING:

Group discussion: 18 + (scores for items 2, 4, & 6) - (scores for items 1,3, & 5)

Meetings: 18 + (scores for items 8, 9, & 12) - (scores for items 7, 10, & 11)

Interpersonal: 18 + (scores for items 14, 16, & 17) - (scores for items 13, 15, & 18)

Public Speaking: 18 + (scores for items 19, 21, &23) - (scores for items 20, 22, &24)

Group Discussion Score: _____   Interpersonal Score: _____

Meetings Score: _____   Public Speaking Score: _____

To obtain your total score for the PRCA, simply add your sub scores together. _____

Scores can range from 24-120. Scores below 51 represent people who have very low CA. Scores between 51-80 represent people with average CA. Scores above 80 represent people who have high levels of trait CA.

NORMS FOR THE PRCA 24

	Mean	Standard Deviation	High	Low
For Total Score	65.6	15.3	> 80	< 51
Group:	15.4	4.8	> 20	< 11
Meeting:	16.4	4.2	> 20	< 13
Dyad (Interpersonal):	14.5	4.2	> 18	< 11
Public:	19.3	5.1	> 24	< 14

Source

McCroskey, J. C. (1982). *An introduction to rhetorical communication* (4th Ed). Englewood Cliffs, NJ: Prentice-Hall.

A.P.A. Reference Page Format

References

*Position "References" (centered) at the top of the listing.
Always alphabetize and double-space entries.*

Citing a book:

Sprague, J. & Stuart, D. (2008). *The speaker's handbook* (8th Ed.). Belmont, CA: Wadsworth.

Always write the last name first, followed by a comma and the initials. Use the ampersand (&) instead of "and" between author names.

Citing a chapter in an edited book:

Anderson, P.A. (1985). Nonverbal immediacy in interpersonal communication. In A. W. Sigman &

S. Feldstein (Eds.), *Multicultural integrations of nonverbal behavior* (pp. 1-36). Hillside, NJ:

Lawrence Erlbaum Associates.

Always indent all the lines after the first line of each entry by one-half inch from the left margin. This is called a hanging indentation (as shown above).

Citing when there is no author or editor:

College bound seniors. (1979). Princeton, NJ: College Board Publications.

Citing a journal article:

Cooper, M. (1988). Rhetorical criticism and Foucault's philosophy of discursive events. *Central*

States Speech Journal, 39, 1-17.

Capitalize only the first letter of the first word of a title and subtitle (except with a journal), the first word after a colon or a dash in the title, and proper nouns (see the example above).

Citing a magazine article:

Gardner, H. (1981, December). Do babies sing a universal song? *Psychology Today*, 70-76.

Citing a newspaper article:

Duke, J. (1981, September 4). Basketball player loses position. *San Diego Tribune*, p. 7.

Citing an interview:

Dussik, D.P. (1989, January 3). Instructor at San José State University. (408) 924-5590.

You may find other citations that are not listed here in Publication Manual of the American Psychological Association, 5th ed., 2001. This is located at the Reference Desk in the library. You may also find citations online at www.apastyle.org or at www.owl.english.purdue.edu/owl/resource/560/01/

Refer to p. 10 for more information on using internet sources.

Using the Internet in Speeches

The World Wide Web is full of information, but not all sources are equally valuable or reliable. Unlike scholarly journals, books or news magazines, which are reviewed by editors or experts in the fields before being published, anyone can post on the internet; they are rarely held accountable for what is posted. Therefore, you are encouraged to use the Internet for initial research or supplemental information, but use sources that are more reliable and verifiable (e.g., a recent book or peer-reviewed article) for important points in your speech.

There are issues to consider when evaluating any source. When using the internet, these become crucial:

Content

- What is the purpose of the text (web page)?
- How comprehensive is the information?
- What other resources are available in the particular area?
- Who is the intended audience?

Source and Date

- Who is the author or producer?
- What is the expertise of the author of the text and/or the creator of the web page?
- What sort of bias is evident?
- When was the item produced? When was it posted? When was it last revised?
- How up-to-date are the links?
- Is contact information for the author included in the document?

Structure

- Do the graphics (visual aids) serve a function, or are they decorative?
- Does the text follow basic rules of grammar, spelling, and composition?
- Are links provided to web "subject trees" or lists of subject-arranged web sources?

Citing internet sources

Since the purpose of citing sources is to allow others to find the same information, it is crucial that you cite Internet sources as completely as possible. Cite the author's last name and first initial, then the date on which the page was created or updated, or if that is unknown the date of the search. The title should be in italics or underlined followed by "Retrieved" and the date you last looked at the website. Then include the URL http/path.

For example:

Guidan, J. (1995, October). *Critical considerations of the internet*. Retrieved March 12, 1997 at http://www.ucla.edu/campus/computing/bruinonline/trainers/critical.html

Identifying a Good Thesis Statement

The thesis sentence is the *central idea* of your speech. Said another way, it is a *single declarative sentence* that states the *essence or argument* of your speech. It does not just announce your topic. Instead, it should clearly articulate what you are going to say about your topic and act as a roadmap.

Ask yourself these questions to help you identify a good thesis statement (if you answer "yes" to these questions, you most likely have an effective thesis statement!):

A. *Is the thesis statement specific and to the point?*
B. *Does the thesis tell the listener how many main points there are?*
C. *Does the thesis tell the listener what the main points are?*
D. *Does the thesis summarize the speech in one sentence?*
E. *Does the thesis tell the audience what you will be talking about (the subject)?*
F. *Does the thesis tell the audience what you will be saying about the subject (the predicate)?*

EXERCISE ONE: In the space provided next to the sample thesis statements, write the letter(s) from the above questions that identify which questions are fulfilled.

EXAMPLE: <u>*A, B, D*</u>   There are three reasons why students should become Comm. majors.

_____   My speech is on how to make guacamole.

_____   How to make a nutritious protein shake?

_____   Many people don't know how to use everything in a dictionary.

_____   How to make a good salad.

_____   I am going to be talking about diabetes.

_____   There are many ways people can stop global warming.

_____   Obesity is a huge problem in the U.S.

_____   The legal driving age should be changed from 16 to 18.

_____   Why you should choose public transportation instead of driving.

_____   Every eligible person should donate blood.

_____   Addiction to methamphetamines is a problem.

EXERCISE TWO: Choose four of the statements above and revise them so they are effective thesis statements. Use the questions above to guide you.

Remember: Your thesis statement is a work in progress. Your content (main points and subpoints) may change as you work on your outline, so you may need to revise your thesis statement to reflect the content of your speech.

Topic Selection & Analysis Worksheet

Brainstorm a "personal inventory" of topics and ideas that interest you or about which you are knowledgeable (i.e., places, people, organizations, events, hobbies, books, TV programs, social issues, beliefs, etc.).

Choose four topics that you would like to learn more about and/or share with others.

A)

B)

C)

D)

For each of the above topics, decide what specific purpose would be best for the topic. (Keep in mind that Speech 1 is a demonstration speech and Speech 2 is an informative speech.)

A)

B)

C)

D)

Pick two of the four topics and narrow them down (by being more specific in terms of the focus).

A)

B)

Write two sample thesis statements for each topic. (Remember: your thesis statements should be single declarative sentences that capture the central idea of your topic and unify its main points.)

A)

B)

Comm
Service

Benefits

| Politics |
| Elections |
| Education |
| Abortion |
| Death Penalty |

Speech #1: Demonstration

My Speech Date: 3/1/10 _____

Purpose of Assignment:

The primary purpose of demonstration speaking is to help **clarify a complex process**, idea or event for your audience. In other words, you are to demonstrate (or teach us) how to do something; what you choose to demonstrate can be as simple or as complicated as you like, however: (1) it should speak to issues of social, community or cultural relevance, and (2) it should be something that your audience will find meaningful (i.e., something they might actually be able to do or want to do upon hearing your speech). In other words, you should teach your audience how to do something that will help them better engage in their community, that will help them make a positive difference, or that will help them develop a clearer understanding of the diverse cultures that comprise their community. Keep in mind that effective use of visual aids will likely help your audience better understand and learn what you choose to demonstrate. Your grade will be based on the following:

Speech:

- ◆ Your topic should be socially significant, informative and challenging to this audience.
- ◆ The speech should be approximately 5 minutes.
- ◆ The introduction and conclusion should be fully developed.
- ◆ There should be a definite, logical connective bridging each component of the speech.
- ◆ Each main point should be clearly stated and developed.
- ◆ Use at least one visual aid according to the guidelines presented in the text.
- ◆ Adhere to the principles of clear explanation. Use organizers (signposts, enumeration, acronyms, slogans), emphasis cues, and figurative analogies. Also use definitions where appropriate.
- ◆ Be prepared to answer questions from the audience after the conclusion of your speech.
- ◆ Your presentation skills should include:
  - ▪ Natural and conversational delivery
  - ▪ Extemporaneous mode using notecards
  - ▪ Effective vocal and physical delivery skills
  - ▪ Effective use of visual aids

Outline:

- ◆ A typed, full-sentence outline following the format of the Outline Worksheet (p. 14) is required, including a reference page in APA format.
- ◆ Refer to the Outline Checklist included on p. 18 of this packet.

On the day of the speech bring the following:

- ◆ Standard VHS videotape; your typed, full-sentence outline; your notecards; your Comm 20 packet, including peer feedback forms; and any visual aids

Assignment addresses Course Learning Objectives 1-5.

Outline Worksheet

TOPIC:

ORGANIZATIONAL PATTERN:

SPECIFIC PURPOSE:

PRIMARY AUDIENCE OUTCOME:

THESIS STATEMENT (A single declarative statement that states the essence of the speech):

Introduction

ATTENTION GETTER:

PSYCHOLOGICAL ORIENTATION (relate topic to this audience):

LOGICAL ORIENTATION (state thesis, then preview main points):

Body

•2-5 MAIN POINTS PREFERRED   •USE ONLY COMPLETE SENTENCES

I. MAIN POINT (state as a single declarative sentence):

    A. SUBPOINT:

       1.

         a.

         b.

2.

    a.

    b.

B. SUBPOINT:

  1.

    a.

    b.

  2.

    a.

    b.

C. SUBPOINT:

  1.

    a.

    b.

  2.

    a.

    b.

Connective:

II. MAIN POINT (state as a single declarative sentence):

A. SUBPOINT:

  1.

    a.

    b.

2.

    a.

    b.

B. SUBPOINT:

  1.

    a.

    b.

  2.

    a.

    b.

C. SUBPOINT:

  1.

    a.

    b.

  2.

    a.

    b.

Connective:

III. MAIN POINT (state as a single declarative sentence):

A. SUBPOINT:

  1.

    a.

    b.

2.

    a.

    b.

B. SUBPOINT:

1.

    a.

    b.

2.

    a.

    b.

C. SUBPOINT:

1.

    a.

    b.

2.

    a.

    b.

Conclusion

LOGICAL CLOSURE (review main points and restate thesis):

PSYCHOLOGICAL CLOSURE (relate importance and relevance to this audience):

CLOSURE/CLINCHER (end with a bang, not a whimper):

Speech #1: Demonstration Outline Checklist

Rough Draft Due: _____ **Outline Due:** _____

I have attached this sheet to my final outline and have included my rough draft.

☐ 4   I have used **full, single sentences** (not paragraphs) on all components (you may use multiple sentences in the intro & conclusion).

☐ 3   I have included, prior to the introduction: Topic, Organizational Pattern, Specific Purpose, Primary Audience Outcome, and Thesis Statement.

☐ 3   My thesis statement is stated as a **single declarative sentence** that emphasizes the central focus or idea of my speech, and has been integrated into my introduction (see page 82 of *The Speaker's Handbook.*)

☐ 3   My introduction includes: **Attention Getter, Psychological Orientation** (puts my topic in a context that is relevant to my audience), and **Logical Orientation** (establishes my credibility and previews my main points).

☐ 3   My conclusion includes: **Logical Closure** (reviews my main points and summarizes my argument), **Psychological Closure** (connects to my introduction and reminds audience why my topic is relevant to them), and **Clincher.**

☐ 2   I have used the correct format for **numeration,** and I have **indented** my points and sub points properly. (I, A, 1, a., etc.).

☐ 2   I have included **full-sentence connectives** between each of my main points.

☐ 1   I submitted a rough draft of my outline.

☐ 1   I have taken the peer comments from my rough draft seriously and have made the necessary adjustments on my final outline.

☐ 1   I have **proofread** this outline for spelling and grammatical errors.

☐ 1   My points are **mutually exclusive** and I have no more that 5 sub-points for each main point.

☐ 1   I have attached a separate APA style reference sheet at the back of my outline if I have cited any sources

Total: _____ /25

Speech 1: Demonstration Speech

Introduction:	Strengths:	?s/suggestions/not-so-strengths

Attention-getting Material
_____ out of _____ pts possible

Psychological Orientation
_____ out of _____ pts possible

Logical Orientation
_____ out of _____ pts possible

Establishing credibility
_____ out of _____ pts possible

Organization:	Strengths:	?s/suggestions/not-so-strengths

Logical organization
_____ out of _____ pts possible

Use of transitions or connectives
_____ out of _____ pts possible

Development	Strengths:	?s/suggestions/not-so-strengths

Social Significance
_____ out of _____ pts possible

Support
_____ out of _____ pts possible

Conclusion:	Strengths:	?s/suggestions/not-so-strengths

Logical Closure
_____ out of _____ pts possible

Psychological Closure
_____ out of _____ pts possible

Clincher
_____ out of _____ pts possible

Delivery:	Strengths:	?s/suggestions/not-so-strengths:

Effective extemporaneous delivery
_____ out of _____ pts possible

Total: _____ out of _____ points possible; Grade: _____

Outline: _____ out of _____ points possible
Peer Feedback: _____ out of _____ points possible

19

Peer Feedback Form

Speaker: _____   Respondent: _____

1=missing   2=average   3=good   4=excellent

Introduction:

Effective attention-getter   1   2   3   4

Psychological orientation   1   2   3   4

Thesis statement   1   2   3   4

What was the thesis? _____

Preview of main points   1   2   3   4

Establishing credibility   1   2   3   4

Body:

What were the main points?: _____

_____

_____

_____

Clear organization   1   2   3   4

Effective use of connectives   1   2   3   4

Sufficient development   1   2   3   4

Effective presentation aid   1   2   3   4

Conclusion:

Summary/Review   1   2   3   4

Closure (clincher)   1   2   3   4

Write at least one question to ask the speaker when s/he has concluded:

Note at least two strengths of this presentation:

Note one or two areas for improvement:

Peer Feedback Form

Speaker: _____   Respondent: _____

1=missing   2=average   3=good   4=excellent

Introduction:

Effective attention-getter   1   2   3   4

Psychological orientation   1   2   3   4

Thesis statement   1   2   3   4

    What was the thesis? _____

Preview of main points   1   2   3   4

Establishing credibility   1   2   3   4

Body:

    What were the main points?: _____

    _____

    _____

    _____

Clear organization   1   2   3   4

Effective use of connectives   1   2   3   4

Sufficient development   1   2   3   4

Effective presentation aid   1   2   3   4

Conclusion:

Summary/Review   1   2   3   4

Closure (clincher)   1   2   3   4

Write at least one question to ask the speaker when s/he has concluded:

Note at least two strengths of this presentation:

Note one or two areas for improvement:

Peer Feedback Form

Speaker: _____   Respondent: _____

1=missing   2=average   3=good   4=excellent

Introduction:

Effective attention-getter   1   2   3   4

Psychological orientation   1   2   3   4

Thesis statement   1   2   3   4

What was the thesis? _____

Preview of main points   1   2   3   4

Establishing credibility   1   2   3   4

Body:

What were the main points?: _____
_____
_____
_____

Clear organization   1   2   3   4

Effective use of connectives   1   2   3   4

Sufficient development   1   2   3   4

Effective presentation aid   1   2   3   4

Conclusion:

Summary/Review   1   2   3   4

Closure (clincher)   1   2   3   4

Write at least one question to ask the speaker when s/he has concluded:

Note at least two strengths of this presentation:

Note one or two areas for improvement:

Self-Reflection Guidelines

#1 Due: _____ ; #2 Due: _____

Spend some time reflecting on the videotape of your speech (and then later, in your second reflection paper, on your experiences with the second speech in comparison with this first speech), and then write a 500-750 word paper (typed, double-spaced, 10 or 12 point font) evaluation of your presentation. What were the specific strengths you believe you demonstrated? What were specific areas of weakness that you believe diminished the effectiveness of the presentation? Remember, it is <u>NOT</u> sufficient to focus your evaluation entirely on the negatives or solely on delivery. You will have a stronger self-evaluation if you structure it in light of a strong focusing thesis statement. If you get stuck, you might find it useful to consider the following questions:

Preparation:
- What did you do to prepare for this speech?
- What might you have done differently (or will you do differently in the future) in order for a more effective speech?

Introduction:
- How effective was your attention-getting strategy?
- How effective were you at establishing credibility?
- How effectively did you relate this topic to your audience?

Body/content:
- How clear were you in your theme?
- In what ways was this topic socially significant or relevant?
- How would you revise your speech so that you could improve it?
- What can you say about the organization of your speech?
- Were your ideas developed thoroughly?
- What was your strongest (or your weakest) transition? What made it (in)effective?

Conclusion:
- Did you clearly summarize key points from your speech?
- Did you leave your audience with a lasting impression?

Delivery:
- What were your strengths?
- What do you need to improve?
- Did your delivery fit the mood of the speech?
- How effectively did you utilize the presentation aid?
- How did you use utilize effective vocal and physical delivery?

Assignment addresses, in addition to outlines and in-class engagements, Course Learning Objective 6.

Speech #2: Informative

My Speech Date: _____

Purpose of Assignment:

The primary purpose of informative speaking is to ensure the audience's clear understanding of the ideas or issues you share with them. The purpose of this speech is to present a **clear explanation of complex material** to the audience. In other words, your task is to explain something that requires a human to explain it. Your topic should be socially significant, intellectually challenging, informative and interesting to your audience; you should make it clear to your audience that they must listen, that they (their families, their communities) will be better for learning the complexities of your topic.

- Your topic should be socially significant, informative and challenging to this audience.
- The speech should be five to seven minutes in length.
- The introduction and conclusion should be fully developed—that is, they should include the three clearly identifiable parts.
- Be prepared to answer questions from the audience after the conclusion of your speech.
- Your presentation skills should include:
  - Natural and conversational delivery using notecards (i.e., you may not read from your notecards)
  - Effective vocal and physical delivery skills
  - Effective use of visual aids

Speech Organization:
- There should be a definite, logical connective bridging each component of the speech.
- Each main point should be clearly stated and developed.
- Adhere to the principles of clear explanation. Use organizers (signposts, enumeration, acronyms, slogans), emphasis cues, analogies, and repetition.

Speech Development:
- Use at least three different types of supporting materials (i.e., examples, testimony, statistics, explanation, definition). ⟹ LABEL!
- Use at least three different types of attention factors (i.e., suspense, proximity, "the vital", humor, familiarity, movement, reality, novelty). ⟹ LABEL!
- Cite at least four sources in your speech. ⟹ "According to"

Outline:
- A typed, full-sentence outline following the Outline Worksheet (p. 28) format is required.
  - A reference page in APA format with at least four different source citations.
- Refer to the outline checklist included on p. 32 of this packet.

On the day of the speech bring the following:

- Standard VHS videocassette; your typed, full-sentence outline; your notecards; your Comm 20 packet, including peer feedback forms; and any visual aids.

Assignment addresses Course Learning Objectives 1-5.

Informative Strategies

Organizers:

- Signposts: *So by reducing, recycling, and reusing, you can limit the amount of waste going to your local landfill.*

- Enumeration: *Three steps you can take to tackle solid waste are first, recycle, second, reduce, and third, reuse.*

- Slogans: *So when trash day comes, remember the three R's: recycle, reduce, and reuse.*

- Acronyms: Remember, there are *SEAS* (*S*ignposts, *E*numeration, *A*cronyms, and *S*logans) of organizers you can use to make your speech better understood.

Emphasis cues:

- *If you've gained anything here today, I hope it's a realization. A realization that this isn't your problem, it isn't my problem; it's <u>our</u> problem.*

Examples: Examples make claims or abstract information concrete.

Analogies: Move from the known to the unknown

- *Just as your car needs gas to run, your body needs calories.*

Multiple channels: Appeal to as many senses as possible, including the visual, auditory, and kinesthetic.

Repetition: If an idea is important, repeat it, reinforce it, and tie back to it.

Using your topic for the informative speech, choose 4 of the above strategies and adapt them for your use:

1.

2.

3.

4.

Attention Factors

Once you gain your audience's attention (via the introduction), you need to hold their attention throughout your speech. You can capture and hold the audience's attention in a variety of ways. *The Speaker's Handbook* presents nine ways in which you can tailor your ideas. Match the attention factors to the examples below:

A. Activity or Movement   **B.** Reality   **C.** Proximity   **D.** Familiarity
E. Novelty   **F.** Suspense   **G.** Conflict   **H.** Humor   **I.** "The vital"

_____ 1. "Take John over there. Imagine what he'd look like with his hair styled and with a three-piece suit, a Brooks Brothers shirt, a silk tie, and a black leather briefcase."

_____ 2. "Do you realize how much fast food is consumed by our student body? Within four blocks of this classroom are nine restaurants, including a McDonald's, Jack-in-the-Box, Taco Bell, and a Burger King. Even the Student Union runs a fast food counter."

_____ 3. "The London postal or zip codes are similar to directions on a compass. The initial letters of the codes indicate directions, and the next set of numbers represent degrees of longitude or latitude."

_____ 4. "A home that costs three million dollars and a breakfast that costs five thousand are disquieting facts to the millions who live in a hut and dine on a crust. The fact that a man has an income of twenty million dollars falls strangely on the ears of those who hear it, as they sit empty-handed with children crying for bread."

_____ 5. You begin a speech on developmental disability by discussing a particular child's difficulties learning; then, after describing the causes of this disability and care for children affected by it, you reveal that you have been talking about your brother.]

_____ 6. "Students who take an internship while in college, find jobs after graduation three times as fast as those who don't."

_____ 7. "A friend of mine had a crush on one of the prettiest women in the freshman class. He was in two courses with her but could never find the right moment to introduce himself. One day in the cafeteria he ended up standing in line right behind her. Because he felt so self-conscious, his voice froze, and as they moved along the serving counter, he felt yet another opportunity slipping away. Suddenly, the girl turned to him and pointed at a selection. 'Do you know what this is?' she asked. 'Y-yes,' he replied, 'that's Don MacKensie. Hi, I'm macaroni salad.'"

_____ 8. "Judith Penley paid the price of a clean conscience with her life. Immediately after taking part in an outside investigation of her employer . . . several attempts were made on her life. Scared and confused, Judith told investigators she knew of no one who would ever want to hurt her. The next day, Judith was brutally gunned down as she waited for a friend. With echoes of Karen Silkwood, Newsweek reports that investigators drew an obvious connection."

_____ 9. "The roaring river of innovation has overflowed its banks, flooding our environment with change. Humans are swimming in a sea of technology."

Supporting Materials

Definitions

Logical: Places the term in a category then defines what makes it unique from other terms in the same category (a.k.a. dictionary definition).

Angioplasty is a medical procedure used to clear blocked arteries.

Etymological or Historical: How the word was derived.

Angio is derived from Greek and refers to a blood vessel.
Plasty refers to molding or surgery.
Therefore, angioplasty can be loosely understood as blood vessel surgery.

Operational: How the concept or object works or operates.

Angioplasty involves inserting a small, deflated balloon into the artery and inflating the balloon, thus pressing plaque to the walls of the artery and allowing for the free flow of blood.

Negation: Explains what something is not.

Although angioplasty is a surgical procedure, it is not the same type of surgery as a heart bypass procedure.

Authority: The definition accepted by an authority.

The American Medical Association classifies angioplasty as a surgical procedure.

Example: Point at it verbally or literally.

Angioplasty means inserting a balloon into the artery, like this [show a visual aid illustrating deflated or inflated balloon in an artery].

Examples

Illustrate (factual): *The San Andreas Fault is an example of a strike-slip fault.*

Clarify (hypothetical): *What would the president's health care plan accomplish? Imagine you got sick but couldn't take it easy because you have so much schoolwork to do. You get worse and wind up in the hospital. The hospital is scary enough, but you're even more concerned because you don't have insurance. Who is going to pay for this? Under the president's plan, you wouldn't have to worry about anything because you would be covered.*

Statistics

Thirty-seven million Americans don't have health insurance.

One in four women will be raped in their lifetime.

More people are killed in drunk driving accidents every year than were killed in the entire Vietnam War.

Testimony

Opinion: *Former Surgeon General C. Everett Koop supports the Clinton Health Care Plan.*

Experience: *Mark Jackson has worked as an animal behaviorist for 20 years and says zoo animals do not suffer as a result of captivity.*

Outline Worksheet

TOPIC:

ORGANIZATIONAL PATTERN:

SPECIFIC PURPOSE:

PRIMARY AUDIENCE OUTCOME:

THESIS STATEMENT:

Introduction

ATTENTION GETTER:

PSYCHOLOGICAL ORIENTATION:

LOGICAL ORIENTATION:

Body

I. MAIN POINT:

    A. SUBPOINT:

        1.

           a.

           b.

    2.

        a.

        b.

    B. SUBPOINT:

        1.

            a.

            b.

        2.

            a.

            b.

    C. SUBPOINT:

        1.

            a.

            b.

        2.

            a.

            b.

Connective:

II. MAIN POINT:

    A. SUBPOINT:

        1.

            a.

            b.

2.

        a.

        b.

B. SUBPOINT:

    1.

        a.

        b.

    2.

        a.

        b.

C. SUBPOINT:

    1.

        a.

        b.

    2.

        a.

        b.

Connective:

III. MAIN POINT:

A. SUBPOINT:

    1.

        a.

        b.

2.

    a.

    b.

B. SUBPOINT:

1.

    a.

    b.

2.

    a.

    b.

C. SUBPOINT:

1.

    a.

    b.

2.

    a.

    b.

Conclusion

LOGICAL CLOSURE:

PSYCHOLOGICAL CLOSURE:

CLOSURE/CLINCHER:

Speech #2: Outline Checklist

Rough Draft Due: _____ **Outline Due:** _____

I have attached this sheet to my final outline and have included my rough draft.

☐ 4 I have used **full, single sentences** (not paragraphs) on all components (you may use multiple sentences in the intro & conclusion).

☐ 4 I have included, prior to the introduction: Topic, Organizational Pattern, Specific Purpose, Primary Audience Outcome, and Thesis Statement.

☐ 4 My thesis statement is stated as a **single declarative sentence** that emphasizes the central focus or idea of my speech, and has been integrated into my Introduction (see p. 82 of *The Speaker's Handbook*.)

☐ 3 My introduction includes: **Attention Getter, Psychological Orientation** (puts my topic in a context that is relevant to my audience), and **Logical Orientation** (establishes my credibility and previews my main points).

☐ 3 My conclusion includes: **Logical Closure** (review my main points and summarizes my argument), **Psychological Closure** (connects to my introduction and reminds audience why my topic is relevant to them), and **Clincher**.

☐ 3 I have used the correct format for **numeration and indented** my points and sub points properly. (I, A, 1, a., etc.).

☐ 3 I have included **full-sentence connectives** between each of my main points.

☐ 4 I have included at least <u>four different</u> **APA style source citations** within my outline.

☐ 3 I have <u>labeled</u> at least <u>three</u> different types of **supporting materials** (i.e., examples, testimony, statistics, definitions).

☐ 3 I have <u>labeled</u> at least <u>three</u> types of **attention factors** (i.e., suspense, proximity, the Vital, humor, familiarity, movement, reality, novelty).

☐ 2 I submitted a rough draft of my outline.

☐ 2 I have taken the peer comments from my rough draft seriously and have made the necessary adjustments on my final outline.

☐ 3 I have **proofread** this outline for spelling and grammatical errors.

☐ 3 I have exercised **academic integrity** and given credit where credit is due.

☐ 6 I have attached a separate APA style reference sheet at the back of my outline if I have cited any sources

Total: _____ /50

Speech 2: Informative

Introduction: _____ Strengths: _____ ?s/suggestions/not-so-strengths _____

Attention-getting Material
_____ out of _____ pts possible

Psychological Orientation
_____ out of _____ pts possible

Logical Orientation
_____ out of _____ pts possible

Establishing credibility
_____ out of _____ pts possible

Organization: _____ Strengths: _____ ?s/suggestions/not-so-strengths _____

Logical organization
_____ out of _____ pts possible

Use of transitions or connectives
_____ out of _____ pts possible

Development _____ Strengths: _____ ?s/suggestions/not-so-strengths _____

Social significance
_____ out of _____ pts possible

Attention factors
_____ out of _____ pts possible

Support
_____ out of _____ pts possible

Conclusion: _____ Strengths: _____ ?s/suggestions/not-so-strengths _____

Logical Closure
_____ out of _____ pts possible

Psychological Closure
_____ out of _____ pts possible

Clincher
_____ out of _____ pts possible

Delivery: _____ Strengths: _____ ?s/suggestions/not-so-strengths: _____

Effective extemporaneous delivery
_____ out of _____ pts possible

Total: _____ out of _____ points possible; Grade: _____

Outline: _____ out of _____ points possible
Peer Feedback: _____ out of _____ points possible

33

Peer Feedback Form

Speaker: _____   Respondent: _____

1=missing   2=average   3=good   4=excellent

Introduction:

Effective attention-getter   1   2   3   4

Psychological orientation   1   2   3   4

Thesis statement   1   2   3   4

What was the thesis? _____

Preview of main points   1   2   3   4

Establishing credibility   1   2   3   4

Body:

What were the main points?: _____

_____

_____

_____

Clear organization   1   2   3   4

Effective use of connectives   1   2   3   4

Sufficient development   1   2   3   4

Effective presentation aid   1   2   3   4

Conclusion:

Summary/Review   1   2   3   4

Closure (clincher)   1   2   3   4

Write at least one question to ask the speaker when s/he has concluded:

Note at least two strengths of this presentation:

Note one or two areas for improvement:

Peer Feedback Form

Speaker: _____   Respondent: _____

1=missing   2=average   3=good   4=excellent

Introduction:

Effective attention-getter   1   2   3   4

Psychological orientation   1   2   3   4

Thesis statement   1   2   3   4

What was the thesis? _____

Preview of main points   1   2   3   4

Establishing credibility   1   2   3   4

Body:

What were the main points?: _____
_____
_____
_____

Clear organization   1   2   3   4

Effective use of connectives   1   2   3   4

Sufficient development   1   2   3   4

Effective presentation aid   1   2   3   4

Conclusion:

Summary/Review   1   2   3   4

Closure (clincher)   1   2   3   4

Write at least one question to ask the speaker when s/he has concluded:

Note at least two strengths of this presentation:

Note one or two areas for improvement:

Peer Feedback Form

Speaker: _____   Respondent: _____

1=missing   2=average   3=good   4=excellent

Introduction:

Effective attention-getter	1	2	3	4
Psychological orientation	1	2	3	4
Thesis statement	1	2	3	4

What was the thesis? _____

Preview of main points	1	2	3	4
Establishing credibility	1	2	3	4

Body:

What were the main points?: _____

_____

_____

_____

Clear organization	1	2	3	4
Effective use of connectives	1	2	3	4
Sufficient development	1	2	3	4
Effective presentation aid	1	2	3	4

Conclusion:

Summary/Review	1	2	3	4
Closure (clincher)	1	2	3	4

Write at least one question to ask the speaker when s/he has concluded:

Note at least two strengths of this presentation:

Note one or two areas for improvement:

Speech #3: Persuasive

My Speech Date: _____

Purpose of Assignment:

In this final speech, you will apply all of the concepts you have learned so far in this course. You will stay with your informative speech topic, using your peers' feedback to craft a sound and effectively communicated persuasive argument. Your goal is to influence this audience to effect change in their lives and in their communities. <u>Your thesis should be stated as a proposition of public policy on an issue of social significance</u>. In addition, you must call for a **direct and specific course of action** from your audience. Your speech is to be based on sound reasoning and evidence and must include motivational appeals; to be effective in your attempts to persuade, you must establish yourself as a credible speaker.

- ♦ Your topic should be socially significant, timely and one that you find very interesting.
- ♦ The speech should be six to eight minutes in length.
- ♦ The introduction and conclusion should be fully developed.
- ♦ Be prepared to answer questions from the audience after the conclusion of your speech.
- ♦ Your style (language choice) should be clear, appropriate, vivid, and varied.
- ♦ Your delivery skills should be the best so far— extemporaneous, conversational, energetic, and non-distracting. Also, use visual aids effectively.

<u>Speech Organization:</u>
- ▪ The speech should be well organized using the Problem-Solution or Monroe's Motivated Sequence patterns.
- ▪ There should be a definite, logical connective bridging each component of the speech.
- ▪ Each main point should be clearly stated and developed.
- ▪ Adhere to the principles of clear explanation. Use organizers (signposts, enumeration, acronyms, slogans), emphasis cues, analogies, and repetition.

<u>Speech Development:</u>
- ▪ Use at least one instance of valid reasoning (i.e., causal, inductive, deductive, analogic).
- ▪ Use at least two different methods to establish your credibility with the audience (i.e., concern, competence, trustworthiness, dynamism).
- ▪ Use at least one appeal to audience needs and one appeal to audience values.
- ▪ Cite at least four sources in your speech.

Outline:
- ▪ A typed, full-sentence outline following the Outline Worksheet (p. 43) format is required.
  - ▪ A reference page in APA format with at least four different source citations.
- ▪ Refer to the Outline Checklist included on p. 47 of this packet.

On the day of the speech bring the following:

- ♦ Your typed, full-sentence outline; your notecards; your Comm 20 Packet, including peer feedback forms; any visual aids; and a standard VHS videocassette (if requested or desired)

Assignment addresses Course Learning Objectives 1-5.

Reasoning Guidelines

♦ **Make your reasoning clear to your listeners.** It is not enough to simply present the evidence (supporting materials). Tell the audience how you reached your conclusions. The audience may come to very different conclusions so you must tell them how and why you arrived at the conclusions that you did.

♦ **Organize your points to show logical relationships.** Although your "conclusions" may be found at all levels of your speech (as your thesis sentence, main points or subpoints), you must lay out your claims and explain your reasoning logically (remember to use organizers and emphasis cues where they will be helpful).

♦ **Use connectives (internal summaries and previews) to demonstrate your reasoning.** Do not forget to write your connectives into your outline. This will help you to be clear about your reasoning, and it will show me that you have carefully thought out the connections between ideas. It will also help your audience to understand your perspective and why you came to the conclusions that you did. DO NOT ASSUME THAT YOUR AUDIENCE WILL ARRIVE AT THE SAME CONCLUSIONS THAT YOU DID. SPELL IT OUT!

♦ **Use appropriate language with different forms of reasoning.**

   ▪ Show the strength of your examples when using <u>induction</u>:

   One case that supports my claim is . . .

   These statistics illustrate a widespread . . .

   Another example that adds to this pattern is . . .

   Although not true in every case, I have demonstrated that the importance of this pattern cannot be overlooked.

   I can say with near certainty . . .

   Evidence strongly indicates . . .

   ▪ State your premises and spell out your reasoning when using <u>deduction</u>:

   Underlying my position is one of the fundamental tenets of our Constitution . . .

   My argument rests on the assumption that . . .

I hope you will agree that . . .

Since I've shown you X and Y, I'm sure you'll see how I reached my conclusion...

Therefore . . .

These statistics mean . . .

- Qualify your causal claims by demonstrating the strength of the <u>causal relationship</u>.

    There may be many causes, but the one I have identified is a major

    cause . . .

    In the vast majority of cases, X has been shown to cause Y.

    In every case I have shown you, when taxes went down, the economy improved.

    For every unit of increase in X, there was a proportionate increase in Y.

    Although not all criminals are victims of child abuse, I have demonstrated that it

    is one of the major contributing factors.

- <u>To reason by analogy</u>, show the points of similarity and explain any points of

    difference that may be important to your audience or case.

    I have shown you how Sunnyvale and San Jose are alike in many important ways

    that will make this work.

    The points of difference do not seem to be relevant for recycling, and I will tell you

    why . . .

    When this same solution has been adopted elsewhere, it has worked.

    In a parallel case . . .

    Likewise . . .

    Similarly . . .

Using your topic for the Persuasive speech, choose 4 of the above examples of effective reasoning and adapt them for your use:

1.

2.

3.

4.

Maslow's Hierarchy of Needs

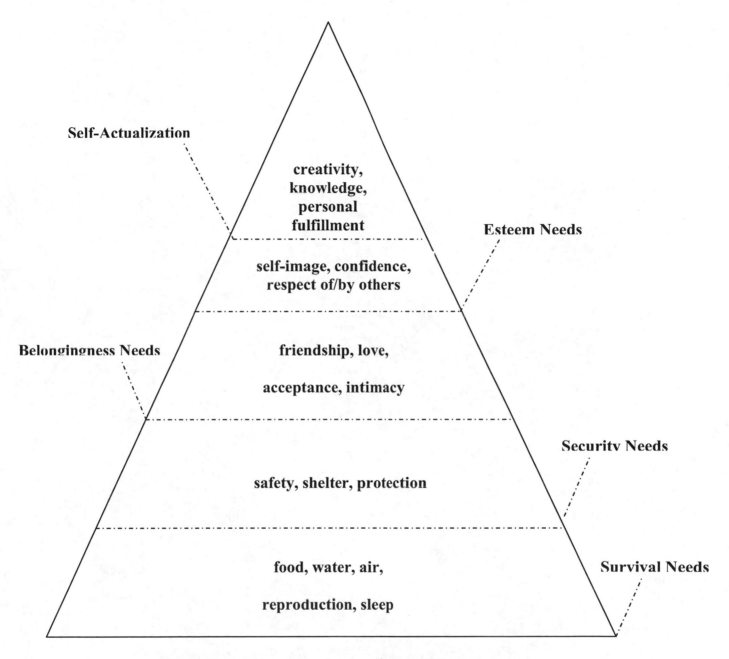

Self-Actualization

creativity,
knowledge,
personal
fulfillment

Esteem Needs

self-image, confidence,
respect of/by others

Belongingness Needs

friendship, love,

acceptance, intimacy

Security Needs

safety, shelter, protection

Survival Needs

food, water, air,

reproduction, sleep

Contemporary American Values

Comfortable life
Exciting life
Sense of accomplishment
World at peace
World of beauty
Equality
Family security
Freedom
Happiness

Inner harmony
Mature love
National security
Pleasure
Salvation
Self-respect
Social recognition
True friendship
Wisdom

Reasoning Checklist

Ask yourself the following questions when you start to develop your arguments and reason from your evidence. If you're still not clear on the main types of reasoning, make sure to carefully read chapter 16 in the text, or ask your instructor.

Inductive:

☐ Are the examples representative?

☐ Are there enough examples to make a generalization?

☐ Have you studied the examples well?

Deductive:

☐ Are the underlying premises sound?

☐ Does the conclusion necessarily follow from these premises?

☐ Have the premises been clearly stated?

Causal:

☐ Does the cause precede the effect?

☐ Does the cause make a difference: If there were no cause, would the effect still happen?

☐ Are there other factors contributing to the effect?

☐ Have you mistaken coincidence for cause and effect?

Analogy:

☐ What is the comparison?

☐ What are the similarities?

☐ Is there a general principle that covers both sides?

☐ Does the general principle really apply to both sides? What about differences?

Speech #3 Tips

Following is a checklist that you can use to make sure that you are meeting the requirements for Speech 3. This is your final speech. That means that I expect exceptional work. This speech should reflect the entire semester's worth of concepts and feedback. Before you present your speech, make sure that you have checked these details.

Outline:

☐ Do you have statistics, definitions, testimonial or examples as main points (I level), or as "A level" points? (You absolutely should not. These supporting materials belong at the #1 or "a" level. They *support* your major arguments.)

☐ Are you using full, complete, declarative sentences? No questions? No phrases?

☐ Have you proofread thoroughly and had someone else proofread as well (checking for grammatical and spelling errors, as well as for appropriate spacing, tabs and indentation)?

☐ Have you cited all of your sources in the text? Do not put a source in your reference list unless you have cited it in text.

☐ Are your sources cited in proper APA format?

☐ Is the *kind* of reasoning that you use clearly identified? Are you sure?

☐ Is there one need and one value listed?

☐ Is your thesis sentence worded as a "should" statement? Is it clearly public policy?

Content:

☐ Does every main point that you make tie back to your thesis sentence?

☐ Is each point developed appropriately?

☐ Do you incorporate a variety of sources?

☐ Do you address counter arguments?

☐ Have you included something that will get the audience's attention?

☐ Have you utilized emphasis cues and repetition to make sure that the audience remembers your most important points?

☐ Have you given them a compelling reason to listen? Have you related the topic to *their* needs and *their* experiences?

☐ Have you summarized your main points?

☐ Have you included a clear call to action?

Credibility:

☐ Have you cited your sources to establish your credibility?

☐ Do you really know your topic? Do you have additional sources to investigate?

☐ Do you address counter arguments?

☐ Are you prepared to answer audience questions about your topic?

Reasoning:

☐ Have you made your reasoning *very* clear to your audience?

☐ Have you interpreted your statistics?

Delivery:

☐ Have you practiced enough?

☐ Are you speaking extemporaneously?

☐ Do you really know the intricacies of your topic?

☐ Have you visualized yourself as a dynamic speaker?

☐ Is your visual aid clear? Readable?

☐ Does your visual aid clarify complex material?

☐ Do you use visual aids in every place where they will clarify complex material or help your audience understand you better?

Suggestions for Preparation:

The largest amount of effort should go into developing the ideas you want to present. Make sure your main points clearly represent these ideas. Give special thought to your introduction and conclusion. These parts of your speech can make a strong impression that affects your persuasiveness.

Make use of supporting materials (i.e., statistics, definitions, testimony, examples). Begin your research as soon as possible so that you have plenty of time to consider how you want your speech to progress.

Review your videotape and decide which areas of delivery to be conscious of during the speech. **Practice aloud using your notecards and visual aids several times.** Work on really connecting with your audience. Move away from the lectern, maintain eye contact, and show your sincerity in your face and voice.

Speech #3: Persuasive Speech Topic Worksheet

1. What is your thesis (proposition of public policy)?

2. What is the status quo (current situation) regarding your policy statement?

3. What is wrong with the status quo? Why do you want to make a change?

4. Whose domain is, or what public body is, responsible for upholding the status quo?

5. Who, what agent, would be able to make, or enact a change to the status quo?

6. What evidence and facts do you plan to provide to support your claim?

7. How does the above evidence support your claim? In other words, how will you turn your facts into reasoning?

8. What might be an argument against your proposition?

9. What are the possible main points for your speech?

Outline Worksheet

TOPIC:

ORGANIZATIONAL PATTERN:

SPECIFIC PURPOSE:

PRIMARY AUDIENCE OUTCOME:

THESIS STATEMENT:

Introduction

ATTENTION GETTER:

PSYCHOLOGICAL ORIENTATION:

LOGICAL ORIENTATION:

Body

I.

    A.

        1.

           a.

           b.

2.

    a.

    b.

B.

    1.

        a.

        b.

    2.

        a.

        b.

C.

    1.

        a.

        b.

    2.

        a.

        b.

Connective:

II.

A.

    1.

        a.

        b.

2.

    a.

    b.

B.

    1.

       a.

       b.

    2.

       a.

       b.

C.

    1.

       a.

       b.

    2.

       a.

       b.

Connective:

III.

    A.

       1.

          a.

          b.

2.

        a.

        b.

B.

   1.

        a.

        b.

   2.

        a.

        b.

C.

   1.

        a.

        b.

   2.

        a.

        b.

Conclusion

LOGICAL CLOSURE:

PSYCHOLOGICAL CLOSURE:

CLOSURE/CLINCHER:

Speech #3: Outline Checklist

Rough Draft Due: _____**Outline Due:** _____

I have attached this sheet to my outline and have included my rough draft.

☐ 5 I have used **full, single sentences** (not paragraphs) on all components (you may use multiple sentences in the intro & conclusion).

☐ 5 I have included, prior to the introduction: Topic, Organizational Pattern **(either Problem/Solution or Monroe's Motivated Sequence)**, Specific Purpose, Primary Audience Outcome, and Thesis Statement.

☐ 5 My thesis statement is stated as **a proposition of fact, value, or policy** and has been integrated into my Introduction.

☐ 3 My introduction includes: **Attention Getter, Psychological Orientation** (puts my topic in a context that is relevant to my audience), and **Logical Orientation** (establishes my credibility and previews my main points).

☐ 3 My conclusion includes: **Logical Closure** (review my main points and summarizes my argument), **Psychological Closure** (connects to my introduction and reminds audience why my topic is relevant to them), and **Clincher** (a call to action).

☐ 4 I have used the correct format for **numeration and indented** my points and sub points properly. (I, A, 1, a., etc).

☐ 4 I have included **full-sentence connectives** between each of my main points.

☐ 4 I have included at least <u>four different</u> **APA style source citations** within my outline.

☐ 4 I have <u>labeled</u> at least <u>one</u> instance of **valid reasoning** somewhere on my outline (i.e. inductive, deductive, causal, by analogy).

☐ 4 I have <u>labeled</u> at least <u>two</u> dimensions of **credibility** somewhere on my outline (i.e. concern, competence, trustworthiness, dynamism).

☐ 3 I have <u>labeled</u> at least <u>one</u> appeal to the audience's **needs** (i.e. security, belongingness, esteem, self-actualization).

☐ 3 I have <u>labeled</u> at least <u>one</u> appeal to the audience's **values** (see page 286 of *The Speaker's Handbook*).

☐ 5 I submitted a rough draft of my outline.

☐ 5 I have taken the peer comments from my rough draft seriously and have made the necessary adjustments on my final outline.

☐ 5 I have exercised **academic integrity** and given credit where credit is due.

☐ 3 I have **proofread** this outline for spelling and grammatical errors.

☐ 10 I have attached a separate APA style reference sheet at the back of my outline and have included at least **four properly cited, credible sources**.

Total: _____ /75

Speech 3: Persuasive

Introduction: Strengths: ?s/suggestions/not-so-strengths

Attention-getting Material
_____ out of _____ pts possible

Psychological Orientation
_____ out of _____ pts possible

Logical Orientation
_____ out of _____ pts possible

Establishing credibility
_____ out of _____ pts possible

Organization: Strengths: ?s/suggestions/not-so-strengths

Logical organization
_____ out of _____ pts possible

Use of transitions or connectives
_____ out of _____ pts possible

Development   Strengths: ?s/suggestions/not-so-strengths

Social significance
_____ out of ___ pts possible

Compelling proposition of public policy
_____ out of _____ pts possible

Reasoning
_____ out of _____ pts possible

Conclusion: Strengths: ?s/suggestions/not-so-strengths

Logical Closure
_____ out of _____ pts possible

Psychological Closure
_____ out of _____ pts possible

Clincher
_____ out of _____ pts possible

Delivery: Strengths: ?s/suggestions/not-so-strengths:

Effective extemporaneous delivery
_____ out of _____ pts possible

Total: _____ out of _____ points possible; Grade: _____

Outline: _____ out of _____ points possible
Peer Feedback: _____ out of _____ points possible

Peer Feedback Form

Speaker: _____   Respondent: _____

1=missing   2=average   3=good   4=excellent

Introduction:

Effective attention-getter   1   2   3   4

Psychological orientation   1   2   3   4

Thesis statement   1   2   3   4

What was the thesis? _____

Preview of main points   1   2   3   4

Establishing credibility   1   2   3   4

Body:

What were the main points?: _____
_____
_____
_____

Clear organization   1   2   3   4

Effective use of connectives   1   2   3   4

Sufficient development   1   2   3   4

Effective presentation aid   1   2   3   4

Conclusion:

Summary/Review   1   2   3   4

Closure (clincher)   1   2   3   4

Write at least one question to ask the speaker when s/he has concluded:

Note at least two strengths of this presentation:

Note one or two areas for improvement:

Peer Feedback Form

Speaker: _____   Respondent: _____

1=missing   2=average   3=good   4=excellent

Introduction:

Effective attention-getter   1   2   3   4

Psychological orientation   1   2   3   4

Thesis statement   1   2   3   4

What was the thesis? _____

Preview of main points   1   2   3   4

Establishing credibility   1   2   3   4

Body:

What were the main points?: _____
_____
_____
_____

Clear organization   1   2   3   4

Effective use of connectives   1   2   3   4

Sufficient development   1   2   3   4

Effective presentation aid   1   2   3   4

Conclusion:

Summary/Review   1   2   3   4

Closure (clincher)   1   2   3   4

Write at least one question to ask the speaker when s/he has concluded:

Note at least two strengths of this presentation:

Note one or two areas for improvement:

Peer Feedback Form

Speaker: _____   Respondent: _____

   1=missing   2=average   3=good   4=excellent

Introduction:

Effective attention-getter   1   2   3   4

Psychological orientation   1   2   3   4

Thesis statement   1   2   3   4

       What was the thesis? _____

Preview of main points   1   2   3   4

Establishing credibility   1   2   3   4

Body:

       What were the main points?: _____

                                                      _____

                                                      _____

Clear organization   1   2   3   4

Effective use of connectives   1   2   3   4

Sufficient development   1   2   3   4

Effective presentation aid   1   2   3   4

Conclusion:

Summary/Review   1   2   3   4

Closure (clincher)   1   2   3   4

Write at least one question to ask the speaker when s/he has concluded:

Note at least two strengths of this presentation:

Note one or two areas for improvement:

53

Introductory Speech

Due: _____

Purpose of Assignment:

This is an opportunity to share a little bit about yourself with the class in a low-risk way. Your goal is to creatively capture yourself in a collage and in your presentation. You are to construct a collage that best describes and presents yourself.

Requirements:

- Create a **collage** of at least 8 ½ x 11 in size with photographs, drawings, magazine/newspaper clippings, and/or tiny objects, which you will turn in.

- Write **2-5 main points** of what you are going to say on a notecard. Include any **introductory** (attention-getting) or **closing** (clincher) remarks that you might include. You will be turning this in.

- You will have **one minute** to present your collage in front of the class.

- Part of your grade for this assignment will also include peer feedback and a self-evaluation.

If you are having trouble getting started, use the following questions to help guide you in your collage construction:
- How would you describe who you are?
- What do you believe in?
- What values do you hold dear to your heart?
- What are your favorite things to do?
- Whom do you admire?
- Who are the important people in your life?
  Do you work? Is it your dream job? What is your dream job?

Please feel free to address more questions that add to the dynamic of your collage.

Criteria For Evaluation:

To receive full credit (_____ **points)** on this assignment, you need to make an earnest attempt at meeting the above requirements. I want each of you to succeed and begin to build confidence and skill in front of your classroom audience, so please come prepared, practiced, and holding you collage.

Cultural Artifact Speech

Due: _____

Purpose of Assignment:

This short presentation describing part of your culture through the use of a cultural artifact will give you experience speaking in front of the class, give your class a chance to know you better, and will encourage awareness of our cultural diversity. Your goal is to describe your own culture or a co-culture you belong to through the use of a cultural artifact. You may want to focus on values, artifacts, rituals, ceremonies, and/or practices that make your culture unique. Consider the sense of identity or shared meaning that you feel within your culture that is not obvious to those outside of your culture.

Requirements:

- Your presentation should have three parts: **an introduction, body, and conclusion**. **Introduce** your culture and cultural artifact with an effective first sentence (attention-getter). For the **body**, use two or three main points (supported by examples/details) to describe your culture (i.e. Why is it important to you? Why unique? How long have you been part of this culture? Is there anything about your culture most people are not aware of? Etc.) **Conclude** with a thought that you want the audience to remember about your culture (clincher).

- Your presentation should be a **minute and a half**. Be sure to time yourself when practicing your speech from a notecard.

- You should practice your speech several times so that you can deliver it in an extemporaneous speaking style. You may use **one notecard** during your presentation, which I will collect.

- You **must** have a cultural artifact as a **visual aid**.

- Along with your notecard you will **turn in an outline** of your introduction, body and conclusion. I prefer that it be typed; however, it may also be handwritten so long as I can read it.

Criteria for Evaluation:

To receive full credit (**_____ points**) on this assignment you need to make an earnest attempt at meeting the above requirements. I want each of you to succeed and begin to build confidence and skill in front of your classroom audience, so please come prepared, practiced, and holding your cultural artifact.

Cultural Artifact Outline

Speech Topic:

I.   **Introduction (begin with an effective first sentence—an *Attention-Getter*):**

II.   **Body (main points in full sentences)**
         A. First Main Point:

         B. Second Main Point:

         C. Additional Main Point (Optional):

III.   **Conclusion (end with an effective last sentence—a *Clincher*):**

References (in A.P.A. citation format) (if you used any)

"My Favorite Thing"

Due: _____

Think of your favorite song, book, poem, story or piece of art (i.e., a book from your childhood, a painting, or your favorite campfire song).

Purpose of Assignment:

This short presentation will give you experience speaking in front of the class and will give your class a chance to know you better.

Requirements:

- Your presentation should have three parts: **an introduction, body, and conclusion**. **Introduce** your favorite thing with an effective first sentence (attention-getter). For the **body**, use two or three main points (supported by examples/details) to describe your favorite thing (i.e. What is it? Why is it your favorite thing? Why is it important to you?). **Conclude** with a thought that you want the audience to remember about you and your favorite thing (clincher).

- Your presentation should be a **one to one and a half minutes**. Be sure to time yourself when practicing your speech from a notecard.

- You should practice your speech several times so that you can deliver it in an **extemporaneous** speaking style. You may use **one notecard** during your presentation, which you will turn in.

- You **must have** your favorite thing (a book, poem, picture, CD, etc.) as a **visual aid**.

- Along with your notecard you will **turn in an outline** of your introduction, body and conclusion. I prefer that it be typed; however, it may also be handwritten so long as I can read it.

Criteria for Evaluation:

To receive full credit **(_____ points)** on this assignment you need to make an earnest attempt at meeting the above requirements. I want each of you to succeed and begin to build confidence and skill in front of your classroom audience, so please come prepared, practiced, and holding your favorite thing.

"My Favorite Thing" Outline

Speech Topic:

I.   **Introduction (begin with an effective first sentence—an *Attention-Getter*):**

II.   **Body (main points in full sentences)**
    A. First Main Point:

    B. Second Main Point:

    C. Additional Main Point (Optional)**:**

III.   **Conclusion (end with an effective last sentence—a *Clincher*):**

Engagement: Audience Analysis
Part I: Classroom Demographics

1. Look around at your classmates. Take a guess as to what the demographics are that make up this class. (i.e., age, sex, religion, political orientation, socioeconomic status, occupation (in addition to being a student), etc.) Ask yourself, "What type of audience will we be presenting our speeches to?"

2. Using one topic from your group member's brainstorming exercise, discuss why this topic is appropriate and significant to this classroom audience.
   - Topic:
   - What is the purpose?

   - Thesis Statement:

   - How will you appeal to your classroom audience? Why is this topic relevant to your audience?

3. Now that you can see the actual demographics of this class, how close was your guess from question #1? What did you guess correctly and what did you guess incorrectly?

4. Do the demographic results affect your topic choice or method of presenting your topic? Why or why not?

5. Why is audience analysis important to the planning and presenting of your speech? Aside from direct observation, what are some other methods of conducting audience analysis? (Please address the significance of audience analysis to your research)

Audience Analysis
Part II: Magazine Ad Activity

Instructions:

1. Select a speech topic for an informative speech...anything at all.

2. You will receive a page from a magazine with a picture or variety of pictures on it. This is your audience for your speech.

    a. Determine, as a group, what you think are the demographics and interests of this audience.

    b. Why is your speech topic relevant to this audience?

    c. How will you present this speech to compliment the audience?

    d. What type of research do you think would help in making your topic relevant to this audience?

3. Finally, create a simple outline for this speech and present it to the class.

Magazine Ad Outline

Topic:

I.   Introduction
    A.   Attention Getter:

    B.   Preview:

II.   Body
    A.   Main Point

    B.   Main Point

III.   Conclusion
    A.   Summary:

    B.   Final Thought (Clincher):

Adapting to a particular audience

Health Sport General Information:

- Open 24 hours
- $40/month (per person); $20/month for children under 12; $30/month with valid student I.D.; $35/month for persons 65 and over
- Pool/hot tub/sauna
- Racquetball
- Classes (of all variety) included in membership fees
- Daycare (extra fee $2/30 min)
- Juice bar and health café
- Personal trainers available
- On site massage therapist (not included in fees)

Assignment:

You are sales representatives at Health Sport (or come up with your own name!), a popular gym in the neighborhood, and your job is to create a sales pitch to encourage

_____ (your instructor will assign your target audience) to join your gym. Using the information you already know about the gym, create a sales pitch geared towards this demographic.

Next, create a simple outline for this sales pitch and present it to the class. You may want to use your imagination and create a performance or commercial! Every person in your group is required to speak.

Finally, as you watch the other groups present, try to discern their target audience. Are they senior citizens, parents with young children, high school students, working professionals (who work long hours), or people who like to work out at home (i.e., video workout)? Can you guess?

Introduction

Attention Getter:

How many of you like to relax on a beach?
How many of you want to look good on a beach or show off your abs.

Preview:

Body

I. (1st Main Point)

II. (2nd Main Point)

III. (3rd Main Point)

Conclusion

Summary:

Clincher (a call to action):

Outlining Workshop

Due: _____

This engagement is designed to provide you with classroom time to work on developing your demonstration speech outlines. In addition to meeting the basic components of your demonstration speech outline, you will also be introduced to other components of outlining that will help you develop your outlines for Speech 2 (informative) and Speech 3 (persuasive).

Procedure:

- Please turn in one copy of your rough outline to the instructor at the beginning of the workshop.

- In groups of **three**, trade your demonstration rough outlines and provide peer feedback using the supplied peer feedback form. Please adhere to the principles of **constructive feedback** as stated in your text and discussed in class. You will trade outlines twice so that each person should complete **two** peer feedback forms.

  o **Note:** It is okay to write comments on your group members' rough outlines to visually convey feedback (this is why you were required to supply **two** copies of your rough outline).

  o Please make sure that the **name of the reviewer** (person providing feedback) is in the **upper left** corner of the feedback form and the **name of the person being reviewed** in the **upper right** corner.

- Take 5-7 minutes to verbally share your feedback with your group members (this is a good time to ask the instructor questions as well).

- Share with the class **one or two** things your group learned by going through the process of peer feedback.

Criteria for Evaluation:

Two copies of rough outline: _____ points
Peer feedback form #1: _____ points
Peer feedback form #2: _____ points
Verbal reflection: _____ points
Total: _____ points

Peer Feedback Form #1

1= missing   2= average   3= good   4= excellent

1. The author uses full-single sentences on all points contained in the Body.
   1   2   3   4
2. The author included, prior to the introduction: **Topic, Organizational Pattern, Specific Purpose, Primary Audience Outcome**, and a **Thesis Statement**.
   1   2   3   4
3. The **Thesis Statement** is a **single declarative sentence** and has been integrated into the introduction.
   1   2   3   4
4. The introduction includes an *effective* **Attention Getter.**
   1   2   3   4
5. The introduction includes **Psychological Orientation**, which puts the topic into a context that is relevant to the audience.
   1   2   3   4
6. The introduction includes **Logical Orientation**, which establishes credibility and previews the main points.
   1   2   3   4
7. There are **at least two** and **no more than 5** main points.
   1   2   3   4
8. The points are **logically organized** and **mutually exclusive.**
   1   2   3   4
9. The author uses **full-sentence connectives** between each main point.
   1   2   3   4
10. The author follows the correct format for **numeration and indentation** (I, A, 1, a, etc.).
    1   2   3   4
11. The conclusion includes **Logical Closure**, which review the main points.
    1   2   3   4
12. The conclusion includes **Psychological Closure**, which connects to the introduction and reminds the audience why the topic is relevant to them.
    1   2   3   4

Written feedback:

1. Overall, what are three strengths or things you like about this outline?

2. What advice do you have for the author about areas of the outline that could use improvement (organization, development, relevance, etc.)?

Peer Feedback Form #2

1= missing   2= average   3= good   4= excellent

1. The author uses full-single sentences on all points contained in the Body.
       1   2   3   4

2. The author included, prior to the introduction: **Topic**, **Organizational Pattern**, **Specific Purpose**, **Primary Audience Outcome**, and a **Thesis Statement**.
       1   2   3   4

3. The **Thesis Statement** is a **single declarative sentence** and has been integrated into the introduction.
       1   2   3   4

4. The introduction includes an *effective* **Attention Getter.**
       1   2   3   4

5. The introduction includes **Psychological Orientation**, which puts the topic into a context that is relevant to the audience.
       1   2   3   4

6. The introduction includes **Logical Orientation**, which establishes credibility and previews the main points.
       1   2   3   4

7. There are **at least two** and **no more than 5** main points.
       1   2   3   4

8. The points are **logically organized** and **mutually exclusive.**
       1   2   3   4

9. The author uses **full-sentence connectives** between each main point.
       1   2   3   4

10. The author follows the correct format for **numeration and indentation** (I, A, 1, a, etc.).
        1   2   3   4

11. The conclusion includes **Logical Closure**, which review the main points.
        1   2   3   4

12. The conclusion includes **Psychological Closure**, which connects to the introduction and reminds the audience why the topic is relevant to them.
        1   2   3   4

Written feedback:

1. Overall, what are three strengths or things you like about this outline?

2. What advice do you have for the author about areas of the outline that could use improvement (organization, development, relevance, etc.)?

Oral Interpretation

Due: _____

In this activity, you can share a story, poetry, lyrics to a song (you can sing them if you wish), a monologue, and much more. You may use original work (something you have written) or the work of another. Your role will be that of the *interpreter* who acts as the liaison between the author of your chosen piece and your audience. This activity will provide you with an opportunity to explore the use of voice, facial expressions, movement, and gestures.

Requirements:

- Prepare a piece for oral interpretation that exceeds no more than **2 minutes** (this may require you to edit your piece or determine an appropriate stopping point).

- You may select from a number of sources including: original work, poetry, song lyrics, a monologue, a story (this could be your own story), etc.

- You are expected to have your piece **well prepared** (I'm looking for eye contact, movement, expression, and gestures), though you may use notes to refer to if need be.

A **1-2 page reflection paper** on your performance will be **due** _____.
Your reflection should address (in paragraph form):

- o 1) What was your chosen piece?
- o 2) Why did you select this piece?
- o 3) What steps did you take to prepare this piece?
- o 4) How did it feel to perform your piece to the class?
- o 5) What went well?
- o 6) What areas do you think you would improve upon or change?

Objectives:

- Prepare an original or published oral work
- Analyze the physical, emotional, and social dimensions of characters found in your chosen text
- Develop effective vocal control: rate, inflection, pitch, volume, quality, and articulation
- Use gestures, vocal control and body language to express attitudes, ideas, and emotion
- Find meaning in a text as a reader
- Communicate an interpretation of a text to an audience
- Explore another area of public speaking

Criteria for Evaluation:
Performance: _____ points
Reflection: _____ points
Total: _____ points

Sell It!

Due: _____

Purpose:

We are all familiar with commercials, sales, and marketing as a result of living in our highly competitive and capitalistic society. From being bombarded with everything from billboards, to clothing, TV commercials, and product placement, we have an innate sense of effective persuasion techniques. For this speech, you are going to give a persuasive speech somewhere in between impromptu and extemporaneous. Choose a household item to bring to class. Using **Monroe's Motivated Sequence** you will be selling the item for a purpose that is not it's original intent. For example, if you bring in a broom, you could sell it as a mode of transportation. Covering each step of Monroe's Motivated Sequence with one sentence will be enough to receive credit for the assignment, as long as you speak to the time limit of a **minute and a half.**

Requirements:

- Bring one household item to class to sell
- You must sell the item for a purpose other than its original intent
- Your speech should cover the five steps of Monroe's Motivated Sequence
- You will turn in an outline showing how you will follow each of the five steps of Monroe's Motivated Sequence
- In reference to time, you will speak no more than a **minute and a half**
- **Be creative!**

Criteria for Evaluation:

This assignment is a fun exercise in Monroe's Motivated Sequence and effective persuasion. Each student will be given "five dollars" with which to buy a product. Each product is worth one dollar. At the end of the presentations, you will write the names of the sellers you feel are the most effective on your dollars. Everyone has the ability and possibility of getting up **to** five dollars. You cannot buy your own product, you must spend all of your money, and you can only buy a product once.

Outline: _____ points
Presentation: _____ points
Total: _____ points

Example: Sell It!

Monroe's Motivated Sequence

Attention: Motivate your audience to listen to your topic.

How many of are tired of getting stuck in traffic during your morning and evening commute? Well I am here to tell you about the new mode of transportation that is gripping the nation! This is the "Broom-Zoom"!

Need: Listeners must become aware of a compelling problem.

The roads are getting to be extremely congested and sometimes your average thirty minute commute to school turns into an hour, which, unfortunately is making you late to class.

Satisfaction: The course of action advocated must be shown to alleviate the problem.

By investing in the "Broom-Zoom" you will no longer be stuck in traffic or late to class- rather, you will be soaring and speeding high above the freeway.

Visualization: The audience should be able to visualize the benefits of agreeing with the speaker or evils of alternatives.

Imagine how your daily commute would vastly change--not to mention your parking situation on campus.

Action: End with a call to action.

Now that you know the benefits of the Broom-Zoom, I urge you to make the purchase that will ease your freeway frustrations for good!

Tribute Speech

Due: _____

Purpose of Assignment:

One of the forms of public speaking that we do not do enough of is paying tribute to another human being. There are many occasions in our lives for giving a tribute: family gatherings, weddings, graduations, retirements, special birthdays, etc. This presentation will give you an opportunity to practice such a speech.

Requirements:

- Pick a person to honor: a friend, family member, co-worker, coach, etc. Share three **specific** things about this individual (your three main points).

- Your speech should have **three parts--an introduction, body, and conclusion**.

- The introduction should begin with an **attention-getter** and include a **preview** of the three things you will be sharing about the person.

- The body should discuss the three important things about this person, devoting a main point to each.

- The conclusion should summarize your three points and leave the audience with a closing thought about this person **(clincher)**.

- Your presentation should be **two minutes** long. Be sure to time yourself when practicing your speech.

- You should practice your speech several times so that you can deliver it using a **conversational and extemporaneous** speaking style.

- You may use one notecard during your presentation.

Criteria For Evaluation:

Content	_____	points
Delivery	_____	points
Outline	_____	points
Total	_____	points

Tribute Speech Outline

Who are you honoring?

I.   **Introduction (include an *Attention-Getter* and *Preview*):**

II.   **Body (main points in full sentences)**
A. First Main Point:

B. Second Main Point:

C. Third Main Point:

III.   **Conclusion (end with an effective last sentence—a *Clincher*):**